T0198559

The Jazz Cat

Renee S. Maxwell-Sullivan

AuthorHouse™
1663 Liberty Drive
Bloomington, IN 47403
www.authorhouse.com
Phone: 1 (800) 839-8640

Because of the dynamic nature of the Internet, any web addresses or links contained in
this book may have changed since publication and may no longer be valid. The views
expressed in this work are solely those of the author and do not necessarily reflect the
views of the publisher, and the publisher hereby disclaims any responsibility for them.

Any people depicted in stock imagery provided by Getty Images are models,
and such images are being used for illustrative purposes only.
Certain stock imagery © Getty Images.

This book is printed on acid-free paper.

ISBN: 978-1-7283-4729-5 (sc)
ISBN: 978-1-7283-4728-8 (e)

Library of Congress Control Number: 2020902992

Print information available on the last page.

Published by AuthorHouse 02/14/2020

authorHOUSE®

I wrote this book for my daughter "Omo" aka Brienna Renee Sullivan when she was 1 year old.

With love baby,
-Enjoy-

Renee Sheronne Maxwell-Sullivan

The Jazz Cat

The Jazz cat
was a little soul
She liked her blues
and her little bowl

She went out to fetch
some fish one day
and got caught
along the way

It was a tune
so plain and clear
It drew her near
and near and near

A Jazz tune and it
was that tune, that
made the cars
just make a boom

Her friend she had
the little bird
no he never said a word

Til Jazzy wrote the tune
that made the cars
make a boom

Her friend she had
the nosey owl
no he never spoke aloud

Til Jazzy wrote the sound
that made the cars
just bump out loud

Jazz (she took two step and)
Jazz (Didn't need no help and)
Jazz (It blew them away)
The Jazz cat, The Jazz cat

The Whole Town

The corners but a little place
A little place within my heart
The store is but a little more
But still there is another part

I want to see
Everything there is to see
I want to be
Everything there is to be

The whole town
It is special place I wanna see
The whole town
It is a special place I wanna be

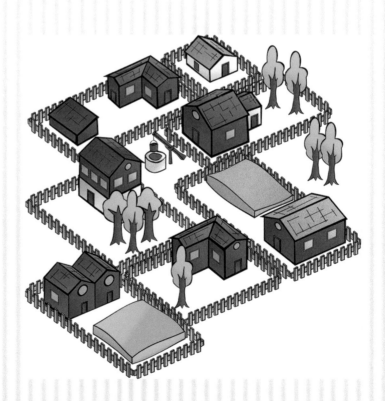

When I grow up, I wanna be
the person God's made me to be
And whoever that is I wanna know
I wanna know, so I can grow

I wanna see
Everything there is to see
I want to be everything there
is to be

The whole town
It is a special place I wanna see
The whole town
It is a special place I wanna be

I don't want anyone
holding me back
And no one standing
in my trace
to my way
Yes my way of living

I don't want anyone
holding me down
And no one stealing
my crown to my way
Yes my way
of giving

The whole town
It is a special place
I wanna see

The whole town
It is a special place
I wanna be

Because I can

I can soar
as high as the sky

I can run
as fast as a train

I can stand
as tall as a tree

Because I can
Because I can

I can sing
as sweet as a bird

I can speak
only good words

I can be as great
As any other man

Because I can
Because I can

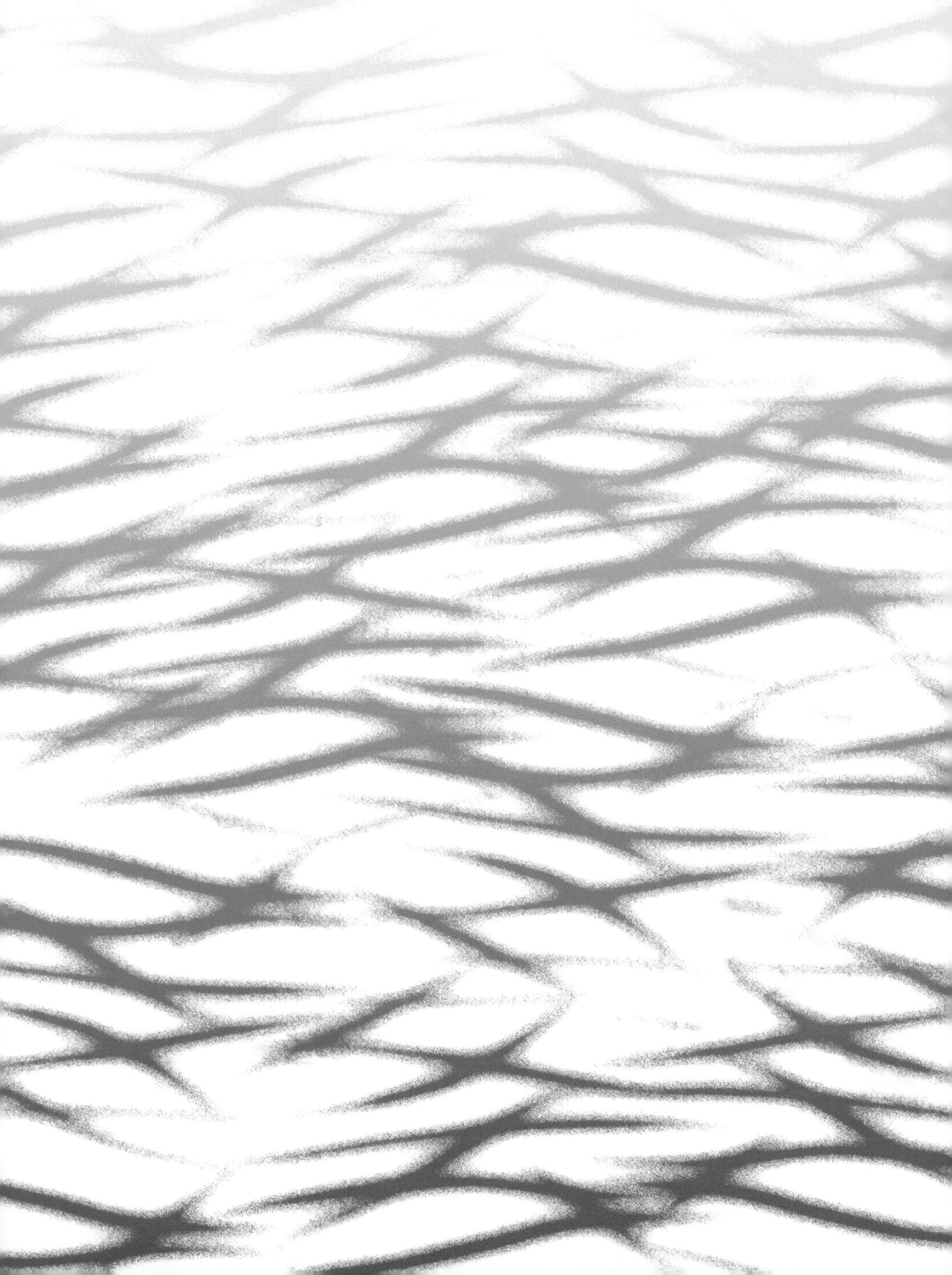

Whose anyone to tell me
that I cannot be

The very best
And nothing less
At what God has
Chosen me to be

And if I should ever fall
I'll remember
I can still win

For God was there
in the beginning
And I know
He'll see me to the end

I can soar
as high as the sky

I can run as fast
as a train

I can be as great
as any other man
Because that's who I am

And it's all
Because I can

Allawowe

Just the other day
I was spending some time
With a little old lady;
A good friend of mine

We were holding
Conversation
I didn't know what to do
She said, "Believe in yourself"
To yourself be true

Allowowe' (It means happiness)
Allowowe'(Never feel depressed)
Allowowe'
Allowowe'

Clap your hands
Tap your feet
Feel the groove
Feel the beat

Believe in yourself
And you will be at peace
God made you
And made me perfectly

Understand this
And you will be free

The Message

The message is from the Christ the king
The ruler of everything
God's only son
the only perfect one

We came in the name
of the Lord
There is no higher place

One day we'll see him
We'll see him for ourselves

We'll see his lovely face
Pharoah, Pharoah
Let my people go

The message is from Christ the king
good tidings
that he doeth bring

God's only son
and he was sent
from up above

We came in the name
of the Lord
There is no higher place

One day we'll see him
We'll see him for ourselves
We'll see his lovely face

Pharoah, Pharoah
Let my people go

Control

How this world
came to exist
And how does anything
Around get fixed

If you don't know what
I'm talking about
Just let the love of God
take control

Control
Nothing but the love of God
Is in control
Control
Nothing but the love of God

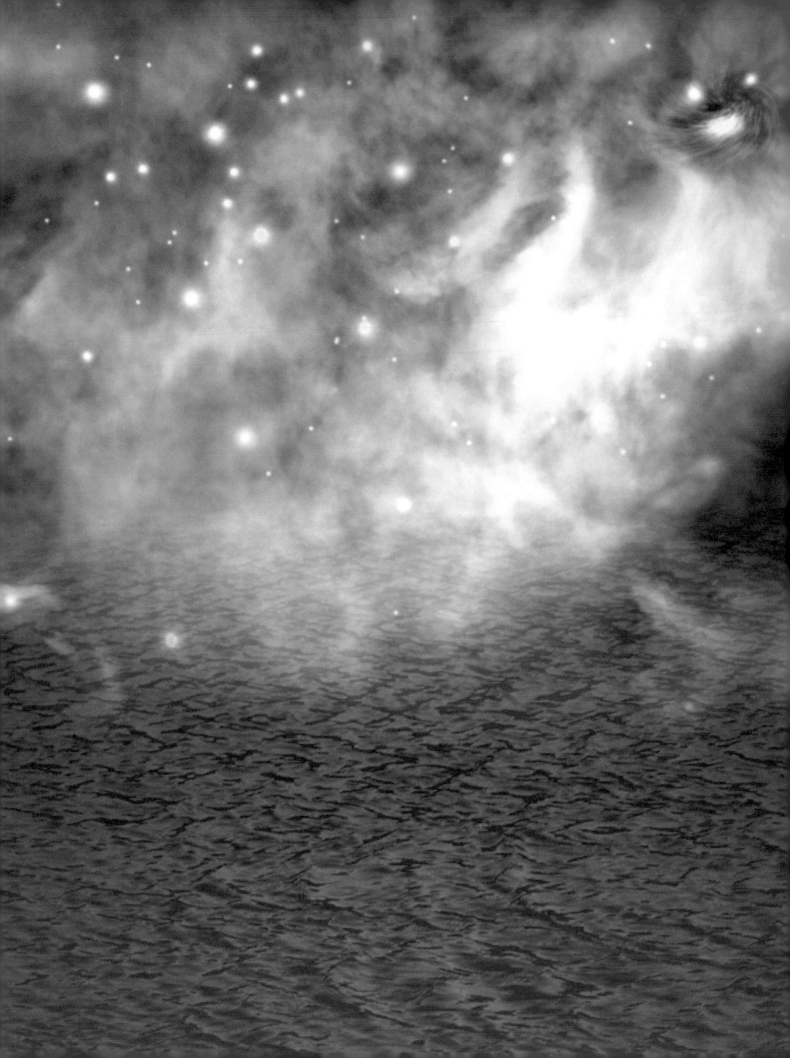

I know you've wondered
About the clouds
the moon and how
the wind passes us by

If you don't know what
I'm talking about
Just let the love of God
take control

Oh, Control
nothing but the
Love of God
is in control
Nothing but the love of God

It's Just the Rain

It's just the rain
Let's go outside

Come on children
Let's take a ride

But we'll go back
inside

It's just the rain
It's just the rain

It's just the rain
outside today

Come on children
Let's go and play

But we'll go back
inside

It's just the rain
It's just the rain

Over the Rainbow

Look at the dew on the grass
It compliments the ground at mass
And look at the stars
in the sky
They make you wonder how and why?

And what is on the other side?
I want to know what's on the other
side of the rainbow

There's always something
piercing me
That makes me want to run and see

I know that my God
Don't make mistakes
And there's nothing
that he can't erase

So let us all be happy
with what we have here

Let us fill our hearts
with love
And warm our thoughts
with joy and cheer

Over the rainbow
The stars, the moon, and
the clouds above;
They compliment each
and everyone down here

I'd love to see
what is over there
but over here
Is just as fair
And it's clear

That if God had wanted
us over there
He would've made some stars
in the air

I know that my God
don't make mistakes
And there's nothing
that he can't erase

So let us all be happy
with what we have here
Let us fill our hearts
with love
And warm our thoughts
with joy and cheer

Over the rainbow

Mission Impossible

I am a servant
Servant of the most high God
He honors
more than hate
this thing he calls pure love

He is about a mission
A mission their seems undone
for the world is so full of hate

All we need is love
we need love
we need love

Printed in the United States
By Bookmasters